D1525203

HOLOCAUST BIOGRAPHIES

Hermann Göring
Hitler's Second-in-Command

Fred Ramen

THE ROSEN PUBLISHING GROUP, INC.
NEW YORK

Published in 2000 by The Rosen Publishing Group, Inc.
29 East 21st Street, New York, NY 10010

Library of Congress Cataloging-in-Publication Data

Ramen, Fred.
 Hermann Göring: Hitler's second-in-command / Fred Ramen. — 1st ed.
  p. cm. (Holocaust biographies)
 Includes bibliographical references and index.
 Summary: Chronicles the life of the powerful member of the Nazi Party who was second-in-command to Adolf Hitler and leader of the German Air Force during World War II.
  ISBN 0-8239-3307-5
  1. Göring, Hermann, 1893–1946—Juvenile literature. 2. Nazi—Biographies—Juvenile literature. 3. Antisemitism—Germany—History—20th century—Juvenile literature. 4. War criminals—Germany—Biography—Juvenile literature. 5. Germany—Luftwaffe—Biography—Juvenile literature. [1. Göring, Hermann, 1893–1946. 2. Nazis. 3. War criminals. 4. World War 1939-1945. 5. Holocaust, Jewish (1939-1945).] I. Title. II. Series.
  DD247. G6 R36 2000
  943.086'092—dc21
                                                    00-008568

Manufactured in the United States of America

Contents

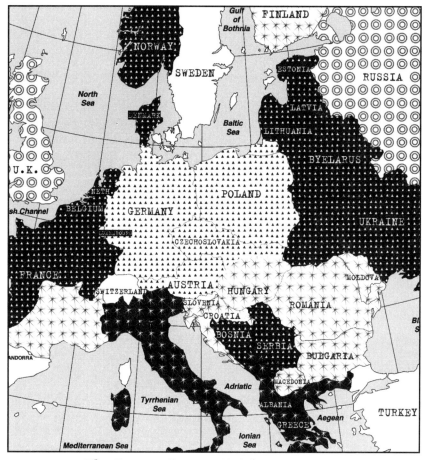

The Greater German Reich (1939–1945)

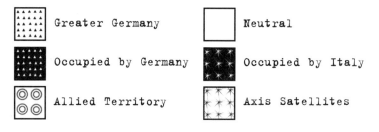

Greater Germany

Neutral

Occupied by Germany

Occupied by Italy

Allied Territory

Axis Satellites

Introduction

On a rainy day in October 1946, at an anonymous bend in the road somewhere on the outskirts of Munich, Germany, a group of Allied soldiers slowly poured several containers of ashes into the gutter. These ashes were all that remained of several men who had been the heads of the Third Reich—Nazi Germany—witnesses and active participants in the bloodiest war in history. As the leaders of Germany during World War II, they all shared responsibility for the Holocaust, the mass murder of millions of people for no other reason than that they were Jews. Among the men whose ashes were dumped into the gutter that morning was Hermann Göring, Hitler's one-time second-in-command, the highest ranking Nazi to be tried by the victorious Allies after the war for crimes against humanity.

Six million Jews were killed by the Nazis during World War II. It was the result of the hatred of one man—Adolf Hitler—who rose to absolute power in Germany and was able to put the resources of an entire nation behind his fanatical obsessions. How did this man, a failed artist and one-time corporal in the German army, become a dictator? How did he come so close to conquering all of Europe? And what, ultimately, led to the downfall of his murderous Third Reich?

One man—Hermann Göring—was with Hitler from his beginnings as a minor politician in Munich to his triumph as commander of the German army. Soldier, politician, and general, Göring was an important and influential member of the Nazi Party who did more to bring about both its successes and its ultimate failure than any other man.

1. Early Life

Hermann Wilhelm Göring was born in Rosenheim, Bavaria (part of southern Germany) on January 1, 1893. His father, Heinrich, was a diplomat who served in the German colony of Southwest Africa and was also the German ambassador to Haiti. Because his father was often outside of Germany, Hermann grew up without him, living in the castle of his godfather, Dr. Ritter Hermann von Epenstein.

Germany had existed as a unified country for only twenty-two years when Hermann was born. Many Germans during this time had become intensely patriotic. They were interested in their country's history during the Middle Ages, the time of knights and castles, and in the ancient German and Norse myths.

The operas of Richard Wagner (1813-1883), most of which are based on these legends, were very popular. Göring grew up longing to be a knight like in the old stories.

As a boy he was very active. He enjoyed all kinds of outdoor sports, hunting and mountain-climbing most of all. Even as a teenager he displayed no fear of heights—as he would show later when he became a pilot.

World War I and Aftermath

In 1914, Germany declared war against France, Britain, and Russia. Göring, who had gone to military school, became a lieutenant in the German army. He was wounded early in the war and sent home to recuperate. During this time an old friend visited him, telling him about the new air force the Germans were building. Göring resolved to become a pilot like his friend.

Airplanes were still a new invention then, and the battles between them, called

Aerial dogfight over western
front during World War I

dogfights, were very risky matters. Göring
proved to be a natural pilot, though, and was
decorated for bravery several times. In 1918, he
became the commander of the squadron
founded by Germany's greatest ace, Baron
Manfred von Richthofen—the "Red Baron."

On November 11, 1918, after four years of
bloody struggle, Germany surrendered to the
Allies—Britain, France, and the United States,

which had declared war on Germany in 1917. The treaty that ended the war, the Treaty of Versailles, imposed harsh terms upon Germany. The Germans lost all of their overseas colonies and had to surrender territory that had been part of Germany to France and Poland. The Germans were forbidden to have a large army or to defend a region bordering the Rhine river—the Rhineland—that was the heart of their industry. They had to pay five billion marks (over one billion dollars) to the Allies as reparations, or payment, for starting the war.

Many Germans were bitter over the terms of the treaty. Before the war, they had been one of the most powerful nations in the world. But now their country lay in ruins. There had been widespread starvation during the war as a result of a blockade by the British. The Treaty of Versailles made it difficult to accept defeat, especially for former soldiers, who had fought hard under terrible conditions for the entire war. Even though by 1918 Germany was no longer capable of continuing the war, and the generals had wanted to surrender even earlier than the government, many people felt that the new, democratic government had "stabbed the army in the back," by negotiating a harsh peace instead of fighting on.

Göring was one of those people. He found it difficult to get by after the war. Unable to make a living in Germany, he went to Denmark and Sweden, where he found work as a barnstormer—a daredevil pilot who performs stunts with his airplane—and as a pilot. One day in 1920, a Swedish nobleman, Count Eric von Rosen, asked Göring to fly him to his castle. The weather was extremely bad, but Göring took him anyway. At the castle, he met the Count's daughter, Carin von Flacknow, and fell instantly in love.

Carin, an extremely beautiful and outgoing woman, was already married and had a son. But she fell in love with Göring—whom she thought of as one of the German heroes of myth and legend—which caused a scandal in

Adolf Hitler was born in Austria in 1889. As a boy, he wanted to become an artist, but he was unable to get into art school in Vienna, the capital of Austria. For several years he lived there in poverty, barely able to make a living.

When the war came, Hitler, though an Austrian, joined the German army. He served as a dispatch-runner, carrying messages to and from the front, and was decorated for bravery. Like Göring, he was bitter about the end of the war. In Munich, he had taken over a small political party, which he renamed the National Socialist German Workers' Party (known by its German initials, NSDAP)—the Nazis.

Hitler hated democracy, communism, and especially the Jews, whom he blamed for the defeat of Germany. He wanted to overthrow the German Republic and establish a new government that would purge the country of foreigners and Jews, and be governed by a single, strong leader (führer)—himself. He spoke openly about tearing up the Versailles treaty and rearming Germany, which made him very popular.

Sweden. She eventually divorced her husband and married Göring in Munich in 1922, where his fortunes had suddenly changed.

Hitler wanted to purge Germany
of all foreigners and Jews.

He had returned to the Bavarian capital to attend the university there. But he had also met a man who would dominate his life for the next twenty-four years: Adolf Hitler.

Upheaval and Exile

Göring was soon under the sway of the magnetic Hitler. Göring swore an oath of loyalty to Hitler. Hitler, pleased to have a soldier of Göring's reputation in the Nazi Party, made Göring the

13

This anti-Nazi cartoon depicts Hitler
goading Brownshirts into action.

head of the *Sturmabteilung* (SA), also known as
the Storm Troopers, or Brownshirts. This was a
rowdy collection of thugs and petty criminals
used to protect Party members, as well as to
attack other political parties and groups.

In 1923, Hitler felt that the time was ripe to
strike against the government. Bavaria was in a
state of upheaval; the local government was
trying to separate itself from the rest of Germany
and become independent. At a rally held by the

separatists in the Bürgerbräukeller beer hall in Munich, Hitler and Göring, backed by the SA, captured the heads of the Bavarian government and proclaimed a new German state.

Hitler planned to win over the army's generals and then march on Berlin, the German capital. He felt that the army would not attack its own citizens. However, he was wrong. During the night, the captured heads of the government slipped away from the beer hall and called out the police and the army. The next day, Hitler and his followers attempted to march into the center of Munich. The police confronted them and opened fire.

Hitler escaped unharmed, although he was later captured and sentenced to prison. Göring was seriously wounded in the thigh. He managed to escape and fled with Carin to Austria, for he was now a wanted man in Germany. He spent several months in an Austrian hospital, where, because of the great pain of his wound, he was given morphine. He eventually became addicted to the drug.

Soon it was no longer safe to remain in Austria. Göring and Carin began to travel throughout Europe, first going to Italy, where he met the Fascist dictator, Benito Mussolini. Unable to work, they lived off the charity of Nazi sympathizers.

Eventually, Göring and Carin returned to Sweden. Göring's addiction to morphine made him increasingly unstable and subject to fits of violent anger, when he would strike out at anyone around him. He had lost his youthful slimness and began to put on weight— eventually ballooning up to 280 pounds. Finally, unable to put up with his behavior any longer, Carin's family had Göring committed to an insane asylum, where he was at last able to overcome his addiction.

Göring was in an even worse position now than he had been before returning to Germany. Unable to find work, this time he had a wife to support as well. Although his devotion to Hitler was as strong as ever, he was out of favor with the Nazi leader, who, though sentenced to five years for treason (an unusually light sentence), had been released after only nine months. Immediately, the future dictator began to rebuild the Party. Göring did not figure in his plans—indeed, how could he, when he was in exile, a fugitive from German justice? Worse, Hitler's close associates were telling him all about Göring's deteriorating physical condition (he walked with a limp now) and especially about his morphine addiction. Hitler listened and shoved his former comrade to the side.

In 1927, Germany declared an amnesty for all of its political fugitives. Göring was finally free to return to his homeland, which he soon did. He managed to secure a job as a representative of BMW and went to Berlin to be a lobbyist for that company and the new German airline, Lufthansa, at the Reichstag, Germany's parliament. His fortunes were looking up again. Soon, Hitler would once more find a use for him. This time, in large part thanks to Göring, the Nazis would succeed in their attempt to seize power in Germany.

2. Rise of the Nazis

Adolf Hitler had advanced the Nazi Party since his release from Landsberg Prison in 1924. He had established Party organizations in every part of Germany, and the Nazis were growing in popularity. Hitler was laying the foundation for another attempt to take over the government; but this time he would do it legally, through the ballot box.

To do so, he would need the support of the upper classes of Germany, especially the aristocrats who dominated the command of the army as well as the major industries. But Hitler, like most of the leadership of the Nazi Party, was from a middle-class background; he had no contacts among the upper classes. He would need someone who came from the same background as they did in order to influence the top ranks of German society.

Göring was his man. Although his family had not been very wealthy, they were members of the aristocracy. Göring had attended military school with members of the best families in Germany; moreover, he was a war hero, respected by the army leadership. His new job gave him influence both among the industrialists and the members of the Reichstag. He was a charming and cultured man, and, most important, a fanatical Nazi who owed personal allegiance to Hitler.

Joining the Nazis

In 1928, Göring became one of the ten Nazi members of the Reichstag. He immediately began to use his new position to help the Nazi cause. As a member of Germany's parliament, he enjoyed free travel privileges and immunity from arrest, which allowed him to spread the Nazi message throughout Germany. He had

This rally in Nuremberg
(September 1923) was the
prototype of official Nazi
mass gatherings after the
seizure of power in 1933.

become an effective public speaker, capable of rousing the emotions of crowds with his hateful anti-Semitic and anti-Communist rants. But he could be even more seductive in private, when he wined and dined the heads of German companies, outlining how the Nazi rearmament program would benefit German industry.

The next few years were troubled ones both for Göring and Germany. The German government was increasingly paralyzed by the worldwide depression that began with the collapse of the New York stock market in 1929. Under Germany's parliamentary government, new elections had to be called if the head of the government—the chancellor—did not enjoy the support of the majority of the Reichstag, which frequently happened. The Nazis steadily increased their representation in the Reichstag in each election, thanks in large part to Göring's influence with the German upper classes, as well as the brutal tactics of the SA, which terrorized and assaulted opposing political

Hermann Göring delivers a speech
at District Party Day in Weimar.
Adolf Hitler stands next to the
car listening to the speech.

groups, especially the Communists, who were the Nazis' chief competition.

Although the Party was enjoying increasing success, Göring suffered a personal tragedy. Carin became ill. The years of poverty and exile had taken their toll, and she had contracted tuberculosis, a disease that attacks the lungs. She died in 1931. Göring never quite recovered from her death, and he remained devoted to her memory for the rest of his life. He now threw himself completely into his work to bring Hitler to power.

Gaining Power

In 1932, the Nazis became the largest party in the Reichstag, although they did not have a majority. Göring was elected president of the Reichstag, equivalent to the American Speaker of the House of Representatives. This gave him a great deal of power, and he used it to suppress opposition to Nazi legislation. It also allowed him to use his influence on his most important contact, President Paul von Hindenburg.

Hindenburg had been the commander in chief of the German army during World War I and was beloved as the country's greatest war hero. Although aged and increasingly senile—he was eighty-four and had less than three years to live—his presence as president had held Germany together as its elected government became more and more ineffective. Only he could approve a new chancellor; this was very important because for several years the chancellor had been running the entire government, ruling by virtue of presidential decree. For the Nazis to assume total power, Hindenburg's support was vital.

At first, the elderly president would have nothing to do with the Nazis. He despised Hitler—who in 1932 was still not a German citizen—as that "Austrian corporal," and he disliked the strong-arm tactics of the SA. But he admired Göring, the decorated war hero; now that the former air ace was the president

Göring at a Nazi rally during the January state election campaign, 1933

of the Reichstag, he brought an air of respectability to the entire Nazi cause.

On January 20, 1933, after weeks of wrangling, Hindenburg named Hitler chancellor of Germany. The Nazis were now in full command of the German state, although many at the time thought that Hitler had in fact been "tamed," forced to accept a cabinet made up mostly of non-Nazis. It was hoped that Hindenburg and the less radical German conservatives would be able to use the Nazi leader to further their own aims. Instead, the Nazis ruthlessly exploited them and created a police state, with Hitler as dictator.

Göring was rewarded for his hard work with the position of minister of the interior of Prussia, the largest German state, comprising about two-thirds of Germany. This would turn out to be a crucial position, for it gave him command of the Prussian police force, which he soon turned on the enemies of the Nazis. The SA were made auxiliary police.

Making Changes

Göring quickly moved to destroy organized opposition to the Nazi Party. On February 27, 1933, a fire gutted the Reichstag building in Berlin. It is now believed that Göring had no part in setting the fire; however, the Nazis were responsible for the destruction, although the public was told that a Communist conspiracy was to blame. The police began to round up

The Reichstag in flames,
February 27, 1933

known opposition members, and the SA was turned loose in the streets of Berlin and other cities, beating and killing Communists and other enemies of the Nazis. After the Reichstag fire, few dared to openly oppose the Nazis.

Under Göring's guidance, the two most important, and most terrifying, parts of the Nazi terror were also established: the Gestapo and the concentration camps.

The Gestapo (*Geheime Staatspolizei*—Secret State Police) was founded in order to replace the existing Prussian secret police with a completely Nazi organization. Its job was to spy on the German people and uncover anyone who opposed the Nazi regime. The Gestapo soon became one of the most feared organizations in Europe, with a reputation for brutality. Arrests in the middle of the night soon became a common feature of life in Germany.

Those arrested by the Gestapo often found themselves in the concentration camps. A few of these had been set up by Göring, but many more were created by the SA. The first targets were Communists and other opposition groups, but soon Jews began to be sent to the camps, where life was brutal in the extreme: starvation rations, inadequate shelter and clothing, and random and vicious beatings were all typical of the concentration camps.

Cruelty Within the Leadership

The SA control of the concentration camps was a sign of how influential the Brownshirts had become. Hitler and Göring both began to worry about how to control the largest segment of the Nazi Party—by 1934, the SA had over two million members.

Their leader, Ernst Röhm—an old crony of Hitler's from his days in Munich—wanted to put the army, the SA, and the newly formed *Schutzstaffel*, or SS, (an elite Nazi organization founded by Hitler to be loyal only to him) under his command. The army, already outnumbered by the SA, would never consent to this

The swearing in of over one million
Nazi functionaries in Berlin, 1934

arrangement. Not only did the aristocratic
generals hold the SA thugs in contempt, they
despised Röhm and the other SA leaders
because many of them were homosexuals.

Hitler desperately needed the support of
the army, which was still powerful enough to
crush the Nazi Party. On July 30, 1934, at the
instigation of Göring, who claimed that the SA
was plotting to kill him and the Führer, Hitler
moved against the SA. In what became known

as the "Night of the Long Knives," the SS and the Gestapo arrested and murdered the leadership of the SA, as well as many old political enemies and members of the opposition. Hundreds of people—perhaps as many as a thousand—were cruelly executed. Hitler soon afterward dissolved the SA and made the Gestapo, along with command of all the concentration camps, part of the SS.

Seizing Power

On August 2, 1934, President Hindenburg died. Rather than call for a new election, Hitler abolished the office of president and added its powers to his own. This was completely unconstitutional, but there was no opposition; the Reichstag had already ceased to be an elected body representing the country. Its members were now Nazi Party members, appointed directly by Hitler.

As the Nazis consolidated their power in Germany, Göring's influence continued to

grow. Although Germany had been forbidden
by the Treaty of Versailles to build an air force,
Göring was put in charge of constructing one,
under the guise of a "national aviation club."
This pretense was dropped in 1935, when he
was openly named head of the Luftwaffe, the
new German air force. In 1936, Göring was
put in charge of the "Four Year Plan," a
scheme of Hitler's that was designed to both
rearm Germany and make it self-sufficient,
which was vital if the country was to be
involved in a long war. This gave Göring
control over almost the entire German
economy. He organized many German
companies, especially the industries vital to
the military—steel, oil, and explosives—into a
massive cartel with himself at the head of it.
Nazi commissars were soon running most of
the factories in Germany. Corruption and
bribes became standard business practice—
and Göring became rich.

Like Hitler, Göring began to collect artwork.
He built a large estate in eastern Germany,

Carinhall, named after his wife, and built an elaborate mausoleum for her on it. There he could hunt animals to his heart's content.

Göring was also in love again, with the actress Emmy Sonnemann. Their marriage in 1935 was practically a royal wedding; Hitler was his best man, and the streets of Berlin were decked out with busts of the Führer's loyal Luftwaffe commander. In 1938, the couple had a daughter, Edda, Göring's only child.

Göring was now perhaps the second most popular Nazi leader; his folksy warmness made him seem approachable and a man of the people, unlike Hitler, who was increasingly distant and cold in public. But behind his popularity, his corruption increased. He became noted for his extensive wardrobe, wearing gaudy rings and jewelry and sometimes changing his uniforms, which included a sky-blue Luftwaffe uniform he had designed himself, five times a day. He began to put on weight again, most likely because, as a result of a doctor's prescription to ease a toothache in 1937, he had become addicted to the drug paracodeine. It was not a particularly powerful drug, but Göring swallowed handfuls of the pills, sometimes as many as a hundred each day.

Profiting from Suffering

Göring's increasing power was built on the back of the suffering of the German people, especially the Jews. In the first two years of Nazi rule, they had been excluded from public office, civil service, teaching, theater and film making, farming, journalism, and the stock exchange. In 1935, the Nazis passed the Nuremberg Laws, which stripped Jews of their citizenship, and forbade them to marry "Aryans" or hire non-Jews as servants. The Nazi definition of Jewishness was a racial one and had nothing to do with the religion a person practiced; under the Nuremberg Laws, a person needed to have only one Jewish grandparent to be considered a Jew.

Nazi propaganda poster
justifying and explaining the
Nuremberg Laws, circa 1935

Publicly, Göring was every bit the Jew-hater that Hitler was. Complaints and threats against the Jews were a common feature of his public speeches. And he profited from their misfortune. Many of the works in his art collection had been either sold to him cheaply under threats of violence to their Jewish owners or confiscated outright.

However, Göring's personal life included incidents that no doubt would have outraged the more anti-Semitic members of the Nazi leadership. His godfather, Dr. Ritter von Epenstein, was Jewish under the Nuremberg Laws (his father had converted to Catholicism). Göring had always admired von Epenstein, who had supported the Göring family throughout his youth. But von Epenstein had also had an affair with Göring's mother, and Göring had been humiliated as a young boy when, asked to write an essay for school about the man he admired most in the world, he wrote about von Epenstein—only to be told that boys at his school did not write pieces in praise of Jews.

Göring may also have intervened at his new wife's request to help her friends, many of whom were Jewish, to be released from the concentration camps. Certainly he was no friend of Heinrich Himmler, the head of the SS, who was in charge of carrying out the extermination of the Jews. But even if he did try to help some Jews, it amounted to only a tiny gesture in the face of the Nazi terror, done not out of a sense of moral outrage, but as a favor to the wife he doted on.

An Infamous Night

On November 9, 1938, in response to the assassination of a German diplomat in Paris by a Jewish refugee, the Nazis rampaged throughout Germany, breaking into Jewish stores, businesses, and synagogues, smashing their windows, and beating or killing any Jews they could find. Known as *Kristallnacht*, the "Night of Broken Glass," the aftermath was devastating to Germany's Jews.

Jewish shop owners clean up
glass from store windows
broken during *Kristallnacht*.

The night of terror made Göring furious—not because of the attacks on the Jews but because of the damage done. The insurance claims that could be filed by the non-Jewish owners of the buildings destroyed amounted to more than five million marks (over $1,250,000). "I wish you had killed two hundred Jews instead of destroying so much valuable property," he fumed. He found a simple enough solution, however: he would punish the Jews for the Nazi attack. All of their property—especially jewelry and artwork, which were coveted by the Nazi leaders, Göring in particular—was confiscated. Those who had survived the night of terror were forced to leave their homes and move into ghettos. And a billion marks (about $250,000,000) indemnity was imposed on them for provoking the Nazis into destroying their property so that, as Göring put it, "the swine won't commit another murder." No wonder that at this time he remarked, "I would not like to be a Jew in Germany."

Spreading the Nazi Nightmare

By this point, the Nazi nightmare had taken a firm hold in Germany. The opposition had been crushed, and Hitler was absolute master of the country. Soon, however, he was to spread the terror of his demented dreams throughout the whole of Europe.

In *Mein Kampf,* the autobiography he had written while in prison, Hitler had made clear his plans to make Germany strong again. First he would rearm the German nation. Then he would add all areas of Europe dominated by Germans to Germany—specifically Austria, although unification with Germany was prohibited by the Treaty of Versailles, and certain German-speaking areas of eastern Europe. Then he would expand eastward into Poland, Czechoslovakia, Hungary, and, especially, Russia, which would be utterly destroyed. The peoples of those regions would be made slaves of the German Reich, and their lands reserved for Germans only.

He had put his plan into action from the moment he had seized power, by beginning the process of rearmament. In 1936, against the advice of his generals, he had marched German troops into the Rhineland, a violation of the Versailles treaty. The German army was still pathetically small; France or Britain could have easily forced them out of the Rhineland. But neither chose to do so. It was an important victory for Hitler; his popularity in Germany increased, and it would be the first of many times he proved his generals wrong.

In 1938, pro-Nazi groups, with the aid of the Germans, seized power in Austria, and shortly thereafter Hitler proclaimed the *Anschluss*, or unification, of Austria and Germany. Again, Britain and France, fearful of starting another world war, did nothing.

Hitler's plans became bolder. He was convinced that the Western democracies— Britain, France, and the United States, which had returned to its old policy of neutrality after World War I—would not go to war with him, no matter what the provocation. After all, they had not stopped his rearmament programs or the occupation of the Rhineland and the *Anschluss*. He began to turn his attention eastward, to the part of Czechoslovakia known as the Sudetenland.

Czechoslovakia had been created after World War I out of the territory of the Austro-Hungarian Empire, whose German Hapsburg royal family had dominated eastern Europe for centuries. The country had a respectable army and an extensively fortified border with Germany, both of which could present a serious obstacle to Hitler's plan to dominate Europe. But Czechoslovakia also had a large population of German-speaking people concentrated in the Sudetenland, a region along the border with Germany. Pro-Nazi groups in this region were revolting against the government. Hitler now claimed that the Germans of the Sudetenland were being persecuted by the Czechs—a claim that was completely false—and insisted that the Sudetenland be added to the Reich.

Britain and France were both pledged to protect Czechoslovakia against attack from Germany, which seemed likely to happen at any moment. Europe was once more preparing for war, a war Hitler was ready to fight, even though the German army was still not prepared for a major war. But Britain and France—though their combined armies were still larger than Germany's—were not willing to fight. At the Munich Conference, the leaders of Germany, France, Italy, and Britain met to discuss the situation. Representatives of the Czech government were not admitted to the conference.

It was decided to give in completely to Hitler's demands. The Sudetenland would be added to Germany. This would effectively make the country defenseless, for the area the Germans were taking from Czechoslovakia included all of their powerful fortifications—

forts that Hitler later admitted the German army could not have destroyed. But the Western democracies were happy to avoid war and believed Hitler when he said that the Sudetenland was all he wanted in Europe; British Prime Minister Neville Chamberlain, said that he had achieved "peace in our time." Czechoslovakia was sacrificed to buy, as it turned out, only eleven more months of peace.

Broken Promises

Hitler did not keep the promises he made at Munich. In March 1939, in response to the threats of Göring, who told the Czech president that his bombers were ready to launch and that it would be "a shame to bomb beautiful Prague," the rest of Czechoslovakia was occupied by the Germans without a shot being fired. Again, Britain and France did nothing. For the first time, Hitler had added a non-German country to the Reich; but as his success increased, so did his ambition, which was now directed at Poland.

Like Czechoslovakia, Poland had a sizable German population; and like Czechoslovakia, Britain and France had pledged to defend the country. Of greater concern to the Germans, however, was the Soviet Union. If the Soviets and the Western democracies fought against Germany—which seemed likely, since Poland had been part of Russia before World War I—Germany would certainly lose, as she had in 1918.

Yet if Britain and France had any hopes that fear of the Soviets would keep the Germans from starting a war with Poland, they were cruelly dashed in the summer of 1939, when the Nazis and Soviets signed a mutual nonaggression pact, pledging not to attack each other. The treaty also had a secret agreement on how Poland and other nations of eastern Europe were to be divided between Germany and the Soviet Union.

Europe was now at the brink of war. Britain refused to back down from its promise to defend Poland if it was attacked, and France reluctantly stood by its ally. Meanwhile, the familiar pattern of German propaganda was being repeated in Poland: Hitler was claiming that Germans in the areas of Poland that had once been part of Germany were being mistreated and demanded the right to annex those regions to Germany.

In the last few days of peace, Göring entered into frantic secret negotiations with the British,

German troops wreck a gate at the Polish border, 1939.

trying to avoid the war most people now saw as inevitable. At the time, his attempts were taken seriously by the British, who felt that Göring was the one "reasonable" man in the Nazi government. However, it is more likely that he was trying to delay the war. Göring's rearmament plan would not be finished for several years; Germany was still not completely on a war footing. He may also have been trying to keep the British out of the war so that the French would have to fight alone.

His efforts were in vain, however. On September 1, 1939, the Germans staged an attack on a radio station near the Polish border, leaving the corpses of several political prisoners dressed in Polish army uniforms behind. Using this flimsy excuse, Hitler declared war on Poland, and the German army was soon pouring across the border. Two days later, Britain and France declared war on Germany. World War II had begun.

3. The Third Reich Triumphant

Most observers gave the Polish army little chance of holding off the Germans. But the ferocity and rapidity of the conquest of Poland shocked the world. Hitler had unveiled a new style of warfare in Poland, one that relied heavily on the Luftwaffe of his most trusted subordinate, Göring.

This new fighting style came to be known as *Blitzkrieg*, German for "lightning war." It emphasized speedy attack and rapid advance. Tanks smashed up against the enemies' defenses, while overhead the Luftwaffe bombed the enemy and held off its air force. A new plane, the dive-bombing Stuka (made more terrifying by Göring's idea to add a siren that wailed when the plane made a bombing run) served as a highly effective aerial artillery. The Polish air force was completely destroyed by the Luftwaffe, the planes often being bombed on their own runways before they could even take off. By September 17, Polish resistance had ceased. The Soviets now invaded the eastern parts of Poland, as specified in the Nazi-Soviet pact. The war in the east was over practically before it had begun.

A German soldier carves his name into a pole, marking the demarcation between Soviet- and German-occupied Poland, 1939.

49

The Western Front

On the western front, in contrast to the rapid attacks in the east, nothing much had happened. The French and British had not tried to invade Germany—even though Hitler had stripped his western defenses almost bare in order to support his massive onslaught on Poland. But the French generals, with the horrors of World War I trench combat in mind, did not launch an assault.

They were content to take shelter behind the Maginot Line, an impressive series of fortifications and heavy artillery that lined the border with Germany. The Line was very strong and almost certainly impregnable from a frontal assault. But it had a fatal flaw: It did not run along the entire French border. The border with Belgium was left undefended, even though it was through Belgium that the German army had attacked in 1914, sweeping down upon the French and British, and nearly capturing Paris.

Hitler wanted to turn almost immediately against the west, but his generals managed to prevent an immediate attack. They needed weeks to move the troops to the western front, and by the time they were ready, winter had arrived, making an attack too difficult to attempt. Both sides now dug in and waited out the winter. It became known to the Germans as the *Sitzkrieg*, or "sitting-war"; the British called it the "phony war."

Hitler had already developed new plans to continue the war, though. In April of 1940, the Germans invaded Denmark, which surrendered without a fight, and Norway, which resisted valiantly but was quickly occupied. These unprovoked attacks were the prelude for a massive assault on the west.

The plan was to attack the neutral countries of Belgium and Holland to draw the Allies to their defense. Then the bulk of the German army would smash through the Ardennes—a densely wooded and hilly region of southern Belgium that was thought to be impassable to a large army—and race to the English Channel, surrounding the French and British troops. It was an ambitious and risky plan, but it worked to perfection. Within six weeks, from the start of the invasion on May 10, to the surrender of France on June 22, the war in the west was virtually over.

The Germans rapidly swept across the little country of Holland, dropping paratroopers behind enemy lines to seize important bridges, while the Luftwaffe kept up a vicious bombing campaign. On May 14, Göring ordered the destruction of Rotterdam, one of Holland's largest cities—even though the city was in the process of surrendering to the Germans. The center of the city was destroyed. Nearly a thousand people were killed, and 78,000 were made homeless. It was the first of many terror bombings that Göring's Luftwaffe would carry out.

Holland was the first to fall. Belgium held out only a little longer. The great Belgian fortresses, which were supposed to hold up the Germans while the British and French

counterattacked, fell quickly to the
innovative techniques of the invaders, which
included landing troops on the roofs of the
forts using gliders. While the British and
French were rushing toward northern
Belgium, the German assault across the
Ardennes began, smashing everything in its
path. Belgium surrendered on May 28; by
that point the Germans had already reached
the English Channel, cutting off the Allies,
who were now penned up in the Belgian city
of Dunkirk. Incredibly, Göring got Hitler to
call off an assault by the army; his Luftwaffe
could easily destroy the Allies, he assured the
Führer. It was an enormous blunder, made
perhaps because Göring wanted more glory
for his Luftwaffe, which had not had a
prominent role in the battles for the west so
far. In any case, his planes, often unable to
fly because of bad weather, and frequently
opposed by the British RAF (Royal Air Force),
were unable to prevent the evacuation of
over 300,000 British and French troops to

England—a crucial failure, for those troops would one day return to France to extract vengeance from the Germans.

France was now almost defenseless. Paris was evacuated, and the Germans swiftly occupied the French capital. On June 22, 1940, France surrendered. The occupied portions were to be governed directly by the Germans, while a puppet state, ruled from the city of Vichy by the former World War I general Marshal Henri Petain, was set up in the south. The war in the west seemed to be over.

On to England

Göring immediately came to Hitler with a plan to launch an airborne invasion of England. It was a risky plan, but it might have succeeded, since the British army was disorganized and in sorry fighting condition. But Hitler turned Göring down. He wanted peace with Britain, which he was sure he could get. After all, France and Poland were firmly under his heel now; Germany dominated all of Europe. To carry on would be madness.

But Britain firmly refused to give in. Hitler reluctantly began plans for Operation Sea Lion, an invasion of England. The invasion never took place, though. The German navy was unable to protect the invasion force on its trip across the channel; what landing craft the Germans did have—mostly converted barges—were destroyed by RAF bombing raids. The weather soon became too severe to launch the attack. However, Göring's share of the invasion, the destruction of the RAF by the Luftwaffe, nearly brought Britain to her knees anyway.

Starting on August 15, 1940, the Luftwaffe began heavy bombing raids into southern England. Outnumbering the RAF by more than two to one, the Luftwaffe wreaked havoc on and probably would have succeeded in destroying the British—except for the blunders of its chief.

Two Fatal Errors

The first mistake was not destroying the British radar stations, which were not attacked after August 15. Radar was a new invention at that time, and the Germans seriously underestimated its impact on air combat. Because they did not destroy the radar stations, the British always had early warning of the German attacks and were frequently able to intercept the bombers before they reached their targets.

The second error began as one of the minor mistakes on which history so frequently turns. A German bomber got lost on the night of August 23 and mistakenly dropped bombs on London, killing some civilians; this was in violation of Hitler's policy of not attacking nonmilitary areas. The next night, the RAF bombed Berlin in retaliation. Although the damage was minor, Hitler was furious; with Göring's eager consent, he changed the focus of the

Luftwaffe attacks from destroying the RAF to the bombing of British cities. It was a crucial mistake, and one that should have been resisted by Göring, who knew all too well that as long as the RAF remained intact, the bombing campaign could not succeed; in fact, he was forced to abandon daytime attacks for this very reason.

Soviet leader Joseph Stalin, U.S. President Franklin D. Roosevelt, and British Prime Minister Winston Churchill

Although London was pounded for fifty-seven nights, from September 7 to November 3, 1940, and cities such as Coventry were almost completely destroyed, the Blitz, as it was called, failed to bring about the surrender of the British. Instead, their resolve to fight the Germans to the bitter end increased, rallied by the great speeches of Prime Minister Winston Churchill, who told the world that the war would not end until Hitler and the Nazis had been defeated.

Back to the Drawing Board

The stubborn refusal of the British to admit defeat frustrated Hitler. He began to consider alternate plans to defeat the island nation. One was already in place: The U-boats, the German submarines, were attacking British merchant ships in the Atlantic. Initially, the subs caused great damage, but the British soon began to group their ships together in convoys, protected in part by the U.S. Navy.

This, and the breaking of the German naval codes, enabled the British to avoid or destroy the U-boats.

Another option was to support the combined German and Italian forces in North Africa in an attempt to seize control of the Mediterranean Sea and cut Britain off from the rest of its empire, especially India. But Hitler was not capable of this kind of grand strategic vision and refused to send enough reinforcements to Africa. The Germans and Italians were eventually defeated in Egypt by the British at the battle of El Alamein.

Hitler believed, with some justification, that the British were counting on the Soviets to attack Germany. He thought that if the Soviets were destroyed, the British would finally make peace with Germany. Because of this, and because of his vision of the Aryan domination of all of eastern Europe, he decided to violate the nonaggression pact and attack the Soviet Union.

Another Two-Front War

Everyone in the Nazi leadership, including Göring—who had recently been named Reichsmarschall, making him the highest ranking general in Germany, and Hitler's successor—knew that this plan was extremely dangerous. It would mean again involving Germany in a two-front war, which had proved disastrous in World War I. It meant invading and conquering Russia, where even the great Napoleon had been destroyed. But by this time, Hitler was convinced that he knew better than his generals. Over and over his plans had succeeded over their objections—in the Rhineland, Czechoslovakia, Poland, and France. He was convinced that a blitzkrieg would destroy the Soviets as quickly as it had the Polish and French.

However, before he attacked the Soviet Union, he launched a separate invasion that was to have important consequences. The Italians had invaded Greece in the fall of 1940, but they had run into strong resistance and had asked their ally for help. Hitler gave it to them. In April 1941, the Germans invaded and crushed Yugoslavia, and then swiftly occupied Greece. But the price of coming to his ally's aid was a five-week delay of the attack on the Soviet Union.

Although there was no natural obstacle between Germany and Moscow, the Soviet capital, except for the broad Pripet marshes, the Russian weather would soon prove to be as great a barrier as a mountain range or river. Not only was there the fearsome Russian winter, with its heavy snowfall and subarctic temperatures, but there was also the *rasputitsa*, the rainy season of spring and fall, which made movement by men and tanks almost impossible because of all the mud. The delay required by the attacks on Greece and Yugoslavia meant the Germans would be exposed to both.

The German invasion, code named Operation Barbarossa, caught the Soviets completely by surprise. Advancing north and south of the Pripet marshes, the Germans quickly conquered the Ukraine, the main grain-producing area of the Soviet Union, and besieged Leningrad. But time, and a miscalculation by Hitler, who had seriously underestimated the strength of the Soviet army based on figures supplied by Göring, began to weigh against the Germans. (Hitler thought the Soviets had an army about equal in size to the German army; it was actually almost twice as large.)

Göring's Luftwaffe became increasingly ineffective. Lacking good airfields, they found it difficult to keep up with the rest of the German advance. The Luftwaffe was also unable to defeat the Soviet air force, which did severe damage to the German army. The corruption of the government agencies under Göring began to affect the course of the war; the Air Ministry was badly mismanaged and unable to make up for the heavy losses the Luftwaffe was taking both in Russia and Britain.

By early October 1941, winter had begun in Russia. As the temperatures plummeted and

A German soldier stands guard
during a snowstorm.

the snow began to fall, the Luftwaffe was
almost permanently grounded. The tank
forces, which were within thirty miles of
Moscow, ground to a halt. The troops, still in
their thin summer uniforms, suffered terribly
from exposure and frostbite. It was so cold that
fires had to be started under the tank engines
in order to heat them up enough to start. But
Hitler insisted that they hold their ground,
even in the face of fierce attacks by the Soviets,
who were well equipped and had great
experience in winter fighting.

Still, as all across Europe soldiers dug in for
the winter, Germany seemed on the verge of
victory. Most of European Russia was in their
possession, as well as France and eastern
Europe. Britain alone stood against the might
of the Third Reich, which now commanded the
greatest empire in Europe since the days of
Napoleon. But within a year, Germany would
be in retreat on all fronts.

4. The Tide Turns

The winter of 1941–1942 was to be a cold one indeed. Thousands of soldiers on the Soviet front would die of the effects of the weather; and with them would die Hitler's dreams of German mastery of Europe.

Hitler's Pacific allies, the Japanese, had launched a surprise attack against the U.S. naval base at Pearl Harbor, Hawaii, on December 7, 1941. Four days later, Germany declared war on the United States. Up until this point, Hitler had been careful to avoid bringing the United States into the war, even when the U.S. Navy had aided the British in destroying German U-boats. But now he recklessly played into Churchill's hands by bringing the industrial might of America to the aid of the British. Hitler and Göring deluded themselves into believing that the United States could not convert its industry to military production quickly—a delusion based on Göring's own calculations. It was yet another misstep that would prove fatal to the Third Reich.

Slaughter in Europe

Although the war was reaching a critical point, the Nazis continued to carry out their plans to create a "racially pure" Central Europe. Immediately after the occupation of Poland, all Jews in the western part of the country, which had been made a part of Germany, were moved into ghettos in the central section of Poland, which was a Nazi "protectorate" (or puppet state) called the General Government, where they were joined by Jews from Germany and the other occupied countries. Under the direction of Hitler and Göring, plans were made to wipe out the Jews.

"Kill all the men in the Ukraine, and then send in the SS stallions," Göring had directed Richard Heydrich, the head of the *Sicherheitsdienst* (SD), the secret police division of the SS. The first method of mass murder used was the *Einsatzkommando*, the Special Action Commandos. These were members of the SS who killed Jews wherever they could find them, making them dig their own burial trench before massacring them with machine gun fire. As the Nazis spread into Russia, the *Einsatzkommando* followed, executing prisoners of war and Soviet commissars (political officers assigned to the army to make sure the soldiers remained loyal to the Communist Party) as well. By March of 1943, the *Einsatzkommando* had exterminated more than 630,000 Jewish men, women, and children in Russia alone. In all, these vicious murderers killed well over a million Jews in the occupied regions of eastern Europe.

But by then the Germans had found a more efficient method of mass murder. As effective as the *Einsatzkommando* were, their methods were too slow for the heads of the Nazi Party. On July 31, 1941, Göring issued a directive to Heydrich requesting that he find a way to reach a final solution (*Endlösung*) to the "Jewish question." This simple phrase meant nothing less than the total extermination of Europe's Jewish population. At a conference of the heads of the SS at Wannsee, a suburb of Berlin, on January 20, 1942, the techniques of the Final Solution were agreed upon.

Even the hardened members of the *Einsatzkommando* found it difficult to commit murder on the scale and with the frequency that the Final Solution would require. For some time, special "extermination vans"— sealed trucks that pumped their exhaust into the passenger compartments—had been used by the *Einsatzkommando* as an alternative to the firing squads. Now this idea would be reproduced on a grand scale.

Across the General Government region of Poland, new concentration camps were set up.

Jews being put onto boxcars going
to the killing center Belzec

The largest and most infamous of these was
Auschwitz, in central Poland; other Polish
camps were Treblinka, Belzec, Sobibor, and
Chelmno. To the camps were shipped the Jews
of eastern Europe, in overcrowded cattle cars,
packed so tight that everyone inside had to
remain standing, with no food or water for the
duration of the trip. Often, most of the
occupants of the car would die before they
even reached their destination. When they

arrived at the camps, the SS officers would check each person carefully. If a prisoner was healthy and could work, he or she would be sent to the barracks, to labor for hours on end, fed just enough to keep from starving quickly. The others—the sick, the elderly, and especially the children—would be sent to specially constructed gas chambers.

These were designed to look like large shower rooms. Told that they had to be disinfected, the Jews were ordered to strip off their clothing. They were then sealed inside the shower room. But instead of water, Zyklon-B, a pesticide gas, came out of the shower heads. After a half hour or so, the bodies—usually heaped up by the sealed door, often with their fingernails ripped out by their desperate attempts to scratch through the door—were gathered up by the *Sonderkommando*. These "Special Commandos" were Jewish prisoners the Nazis used so that no German would have to soil his hands with a Jewish corpse. Their job was made even more awful by the

Berlin,den 24.11.44.

Hauptkasse

An die

Preussische Staatsmünze

B e r l i n

Betr.: 46.Lieferung (M)   24.11.1944

Wir übersenden Ihnen anbei:

		kgr	kgbrutto	BtL.Nr
378	Nr.1/1: Zahnersatz Weissmetall	4,370.0	5,647	1
	/4: Dublee	1,206.0		
379	Nr.1/1: Zahnersatz Gold	0,156.0	5,043	2
	/4: Gold	4,817.0		
380	Nr.2/1: Silber	28,591.0	28,855	4
381	Nr.4/1: Gold		25,157	25,373	7
	Dublee			
	/2: Zahnersatz Gold			
	" Weissmetall			
382	Nr.5/1: Silber	22,950	23,385	8
383	/ "	21,235	21,503	9
384	"	17,633	17,910	10

mit der Bitte um Einschmelzung und
Probierung.   Deutsche Reichsbank
                     H a u p t k a s s e

A copy of a draft list of the
forty-sixth shipment to the
Prussian State Mint of gold and
silver taken from human teeth

prospect that one day soon they, too, would go into the chambers.

After the bodies had been stripped of any valuables, including gold teeth, they were cremated in large ovens installed near the gas chambers. Sometimes the fat from the bodies was used to make soap or candles, and the skin was used to make lamp shades, purses, and other items.

The prisoners the Nazis did not send immediately to the gas chambers were put to work as slave labor for the German war industries. When they were too broken down to work any longer, they were sent to the gas chambers, or shot, or beaten to death. Millions died this way, efficiently and systematically, each step recorded by the Nazis.

Other conquered peoples were victims of the Nazi regime as well. Many captured Soviet soldiers were simply shot—in violation of international law—and the rest were put to work by Göring, along with Poles and those people the Nazis saw as "inferior" or political enemies, as slave laborers or house servants for ranking Nazis.

A Rift in Leadership

As the spring of 1942 approached, Göring's influence with Hitler was diminishing. Even though he had been made Reichsmarschall and named Hitler's successor in July of 1940, the rapidly worsening state of the war was turning Hitler against his trusted follower. There were several reasons for the split.

The first failure that Hitler blamed Göring and the Luftwaffe for was the evacuation of the British and French from Dunkirk. Göring's foolish insistence that the Luftwaffe be given responsibility for destroying the trapped Allied forces allowed a formidable army to escape intact—and now that the Americans had entered the war, it was clear that one day the survivors of Dunkirk would return to France. The failure of the Germans to destroy the RAF during the Battle of Britain was another reason for the split between the Nazi leaders. Although it had been Hitler's order to change tactics from destroying enemy fighters to bombing British cities, he blamed Göring for the failure of the British to surrender.

Now the RAF and the Americans had begun to bomb Germany itself. The Luftwaffe, constructed by Göring to be only an offensive weapon, was unable to stop the Allied bombers from attacking German cities and factories.

Allied air raid on Germany, May 11, 1941

Göring's mismanagement of German industry was now having serious effects on the war. Production of fighters, tanks, and especially, heavy bombers—a vital requirement in the war against Russia—was repeatedly below target. Although some of the more able subordinates on Göring's staff tried to straighten out the mess, the corruption of the Nazi state was too great to reverse. Political considerations—especially the Final Solution—often diverted important resources away from the war industries.

In truth, Hitler's Germany was incapable at this time of fighting a long war. The German attacks had all been designed to overwhelm their targets and bring about a quick end to the fighting. Britain's refusal to make peace in 1940 and the failure of Operation Barbarossa to achieve a quick conquest of Russia meant that Germany was in for a long war, one that it did not have the resources to fight. The Germans lacked the necessary defensive force—especially in air power—to even hold on to what they had.

The final break between Hitler and Göring occurred during the winter of 1942–1943. In the spring of 1942, the Germans had again attacked Russia. This time their objective was not Moscow, but the oil fields of the Caucasus, in southern Russia. This fuel was vital to the German war effort. But once again, Hitler's orders were impossible to carry out. He insisted that the city of Stalingrad be captured. The German Sixth Army, under Field Marshal Friedrich von Paulus, was able to take the city but was quickly cut off from the rest of the German army, which was driven out of the Caucasus by the Soviets. As winter closed in, the German generals advised Hitler to allow von Paulus to try to fight his way out of Stalingrad and rejoin the rest of the army. But Hitler refused. Stalingrad had to be held at all costs, he declared. Göring had assured him that the Luftwaffe could keep the city supplied with food, medicine, and ammunition.

It was an impossible task. For one thing, there were not enough transport planes available, and precious heavy bombers had to be pressed into service as cargo planes. The weather was terrible, and the planes were frequently grounded. Those that did get in the air were often blown to pieces by the Soviet air force; the Luftwaffe did not have enough fighters to protect the transports. In Stalingrad itself, vicious house-to-house fighting between the Germans and Soviets was taking place. On February 2, 1943, von Paulus surrendered his army. From this point on, the Germans would be on the retreat in eastern Europe. Although it was at his insistence that the army was not allowed to retreat, Hitler nonetheless blamed his generals—and especially Göring—for the defeat.

Assault and Resignation

In the spring of 1943, the Allies, who had driven the Germans out of Africa, launched an invasion of Sicily, and then Italy itself. German troops were rushed to Italy and managed to hold on to the northern part of the country.

But with the deteriorating situation in Russia, they were troops the Germans could not spare.

In July of 1943, the Allies began "round-the-clock" bombings, in which the British and Americans teamed up to raid a target continuously. Within a week, the city of Hamburg was virtually destroyed. The Allied bombing did more than damage vital war industries; it also gave the German people a taste of what the war had already brought to France, Poland, Britain, and Russia. With their homes wrecked, and with food and water becoming scarce, many now remembered with bitterness Göring's smug declaration before the war that if any bombs fell on Germany, "You can call me Meier"—a German expression meaning that his name would be mud. Now many Germans were indeed calling him Meier, Hitler being one of them.

Göring made a few half-hearted attempts to do what was obviously necessary—put Germany on a defensive footing, so that, if nothing else, they would be able to force the

This church was the target of one of the many raids
by Allied bombers of the German capital.

Allies to offer them terms of surrender.
(Churchill, Soviet leader Joseph Stalin, and U.S.
President Franklin Delano Roosevelt had all
agreed that Germany and Japan had to
surrender unconditionally.) After the
destruction of Hamburg, he and his senior
Luftwaffe generals had a conference where it
was agreed that Hitler must be told that the
Luftwaffe should not continue to make raids

against the Allies, but instead be reserved to protect German cities and industry. A determined Göring marched alone into Hitler's bunker. Hours later, broken down, he met again with his generals. Hitler, he explained to them, had no faith in the Luftwaffe, and had rejected the generals' recommendations. Instead, he had given Göring a last chance to rescue the Luftwaffe's honor. Attacks on Britain must resume immediately.

"The Führer has made me realize our mistake," said a teary-eyed Göring. "The Führer is always right. We must deal such mighty blows to our enemy in the west that he will never dare to risk another raid like Hamburg." Once again, Göring had deferred to Hitler, even though he knew that it meant not only losing the war but exposing the German people to horrible suffering. This strange devotion to a man who was openly criticizing him at nearly every staff meeting was bad enough from an individual standpoint; but in the second-in-command of an entire nation,

upon whom the lives of millions depended, it
was inexcusable.

Göring had already begun to retreat from
public life. He was fatter now than ever and
was frequently depressed, relying more and
more on handfuls of paracodeine tablets to get
him through the day. Although he never
developed the malicious disregard toward the
suffering of the German people that Hitler
did—at the end of the war, the Führer would
issue orders for the destruction of every
German city—he became more and more
isolated from the outside world. As the bombs
fell and the cities burned, as the German army
slogged through mud and snow on an
agonizing retreat from Russia, Göring and
Emmy enjoyed the comforts of Carinhall.
While millions of Germans were rationing
food, the Göring's table sagged beneath the
weight of elaborate feasts, supplemented with
the best French wines and brandies. His
private zoo, which included a lion, required
enough meat to feed a village. While the Reich

suffered, Göring contemplated his art collection and prepared for the end.

He knew it was coming. Once, during an air raid, Göring and his wife had taken refuge in Carinhall's bomb shelter. "When we win the war, do you know what I'm going to do?" Emmy remarked at one point. Göring did not wait to find out. "Why can't you realize that we are not going to win the war?" he asked. "It is already lost—but the Führer refuses to recognize the fact."

The next year would bring that recognition home to the entire nation, from the army to the people themselves—to everyone, that is, but the madman to whom they had pledged their loyalty over ten years before. The full price of that promise was now to come due.

5. Fall of the Third Reich

On June 6, 1944, the Americans and British assaulted the beaches of Normandy in northern France. This was D-Day, the largest amphibious invasion in history. Within a few days, the Allies had broken out of their beachheads and were racing toward Paris and the river Rhine. The hollow shell of Hitler's "Fortress Europe" had been cracked. Now the Germans were in retreat on both fronts.

Assassination Attempt—And a Plan

In July of that year, as the Soviets drove the Germans out of Russia for good and the Allies swept them out of France, a group of

high-ranking German army officers attempted
to assassinate Hitler. A briefcase containing a
bomb was placed in the conference room of
the Führer's eastern headquarters,
Wolfsschanze (Wolf's Lair). Only the heavy
table support, behind which the briefcase was
inadvertently moved, saved Hitler from certain
death. Although the conspirators had hoped to
kill Göring and Himmler as well, neither had
attended the meeting. If the plot had
succeeded in killing Hitler, Göring would have
become the leader of Nazi Germany—which
might have brought the war to a quicker
conclusion, as the Allies were much more
disposed to accept surrender from Göring
than Hitler.

Only the approach of bad winter weather and
the lack of gasoline for their tanks prevented the
Allies from invading Germany itself in 1944.
Stalled in front of the imposing fortifications of
the Siegfried Line, the Allies dug in against the
cold and bitter weather. Now Hitler unveiled his
last grandiose plan for German victory.

As they had in 1940, the Germans would attack through the Ardennes forest. Then they would sweep behind the Allied armies and capture the Dutch port of Antwerp, the main Allied supply base. Surrounded and unable to be resupplied, the Allied armies could be crushed, and the war in the west won.

It was an ambitious plan, but the generals realized that it was unworkable. The German army was not large enough to smash through the Allies this time. There was not enough fuel to support a drive on Antwerp. And perhaps most important, they did not have enough air cover to protect the tanks from the Allied fighters. Göring had promised 3,000 fighters, but this would simply not be enough, even if they could be found. It was no longer 1940.

The initial German assaults began on December 15, 1944, protected by a foggy mist that neutralized Allied air superiority for several days. Several breakthroughs were made, and the Americans began to fall back. But the tenacious defense of the key town of

Bastogne by the 101st Airborne Division bogged down the German attacks for several days. (When asked to surrender to the Germans, General A. C. McAuliffe, commander of the 101st, sent back a one-word reply: "Nuts!") Soon the fog cleared away, and the Allies began to devastate the German forces with aerial attacks. By January 16, 1945, the Germans were forced to give up and retreated back behind the Rhine. It was the last major offensive the Germans would make in the war, and it had cost them men, tanks, and planes that they could not afford to lose. Moreover, it doomed the defense of the eastern front.

Defeat

The Soviets had spent the fall and winter of 1944–1945 assaulting the German forces throughout eastern Europe. Poland and Romania were overrun, and Hungary was on the point of collapse. On January 31, 1945, the

German troops observe the arrival of paratroopers.

Soviets approached Göring's estate of
Carinhall. Göring and Emmy fled to Berlin with
their stolen artwork and expensive wines,
although Göring ordered one of his
paratrooper divisions to remain in the area to
protect Carinhall. They stayed for several
weeks, uselessly guarding the empty estate,
until Hitler ordered them to the front. Their
last act before departing was to dynamite the
estate buildings and the tomb of Carin Göring.

87

The end of the Third Reich was rapidly approaching. Hitler, barricaded in his bunker beneath the Chancellery building in Berlin, conjured up grandiose schemes that would save Germany. The new vengeance weapons, the V-1 flying bomb and V-2 rocket, would bring Britain to its knees—even though the launching sites had by now been captured. The jet fighters—the Germans had managed to produce more than a thousand—would destroy the Allied air forces; they might have, had not the refineries that produced their special fuel been destroyed by the Allies, leaving the jets little more than targets on their runways. The British and Americans would suddenly grow fearful of having the Communist Soviet Union dominate eastern Europe, and turn on their ally.

These were the desperate ravings of a madman, and nothing came of them. In mid-February, 1945, Albert Speer, Hitler's personal architect and the minister for armament and war production, met with Göring. Over French champagne, Speer told Göring that Germany had only enough fuel to either bake bread and keep the hospitals running, or to keep the army fighting—but not both. Hitler wanted the armies to keep fighting. Speer had decided to keep the hospitals running. Göring urged him to go to the Führer and tell him of his decision, and offer to resign, rather than secretly go against his direct orders. Speer said that he was not going to go to Hitler. He was simply going to disobey him. Later, when Hitler ordered the destruction of all industrial and power plants, bridges, railroads, food and clothing stores, and waterworks—which would have caused the deaths of millions from starvation and disease—Speer again disobeyed him. He may have done so with an eye to the future: The Allies had already declared their intention to try German war criminals after the war. But these acts, by standing in contrast to Göring's slavish devotion to Hitler, saved not only Speer's life, but the lives of millions of German civilians.

It was easier for Speer to disobey Hitler than for himself to do it, Göring told the armaments minister. After all, Speer had joined the Party much later than had Göring. Too many years of common struggle bound the Reichsmarschall and the Führer together; he could no longer break free.

In the end, though, Göring did abandon his Führer. When it became clear that Hitler wanted to die in his bunker, personally directing the defense of the capital against the Soviet attacks, Göring took the last available route from Berlin to Bavaria. It was now apparent that the Allies would not accept German surrender until Hitler was dead or captured. On the prompting of several officers, who felt that Göring had a better chance of extracting terms from the Allies than Hitler, Göring attempted to take over the Third Reich. The decree of Hitler's that had named Göring his successor stated that if the Führer died or was "restricted in his freedom of action"—in other words, captured by the enemy—Göring was to take over. Penned up in

Göring after surrender to U.S.
Army troops, May 9, 1945

his bunker, surrounded by a hostile army, Hitler certainly seemed to be "restricted." Göring therefore sent a telegram to the Berlin bunker asking if he was to take over and saying that if there was no reply, he would assume that he was in command. The reply was swift and devastating: Göring was stripped of all his ranks and titles, and the SS was to immediately arrest him.

He remained a prisoner of the SS for the next several days, under orders to be killed if Berlin should fall. But after Hitler's suicide on April 30, 1945, he was able to elude the SS men who had captured him—they were busy making their own plans to escape—and began to search for American army units to surrender to. On May 9, 1945—the day after the surrender of Germany to the Allies—Lieutenant Jerome N. Shapiro of the U.S. Army came across a convoy of trucks containing champagne, uniforms, costumes, and the fat former Reichsmarschall of Germany, who was surprisingly happy at being made a prisoner. The war was finally over for Hermann Göring, although he did not quite realize it at the time.

6. The Judgment of History

Hermann Göring did not think of himself as an ordinary prisoner of war. In his mind, he was still the Reichsmarschall, Hitler's second-in-command—and in fact, he was the highest

Göring answers questions for the
press during his incarceration.

ranking Nazi official to be captured by the Allies, the rest having committed suicide or fled to exile. He had hopes of meeting U.S. General Dwight Eisenhower, the Supreme Allied Commander in Europe, and beginning one-on-one negotiations on the future of Germany. Shortly after his capture, he held a press conference that turned into a party, with champagne being brought out and passed around. He was a celebrity, and he basked in the attention given to him.

Displeased, Eisenhower put a stop to the special treatment Göring was getting. From now on, he would be just another POW. Göring's Allied captors took no pains to make his stay pleasurable. Once, disgusted at his dinner, he shouted, "I fed my dogs better than this!" A German prisoner immediately snapped at him, "Then you fed your dogs better than the German soldiers."

His captivity did have some positive effects on him. His doctors cured him of his paracodeine addiction. He went on a diet and got his weight down to 200 pounds. He regained some of the fierce strength of will that had made him such a capable asset to Hitler in the early days of the Third Reich.

In October 1945, an international tribunal of judges from the Allied powers began a trial of the captured Nazi leaders. Göring was charged with violation of international law and treaties, of war crimes, and of crimes against humanity. The result of the trial was a foregone conclusion, he knew, but he was determined to make a good showing of it.

Hermann Göring, the highest-ranking Nazi in the world, used this dubious honor, and his status as the number one defendant, to bully the other prisoners. He tried to get them to put on a joint defense. Some would not; Albert Speer, who knew he had a good chance to escape death, denounced him to the court, and for a time Göring was kept separate from the others.

By all accounts, Göring gave an impressive defense. He refused to crack under cross-examination, as some of the

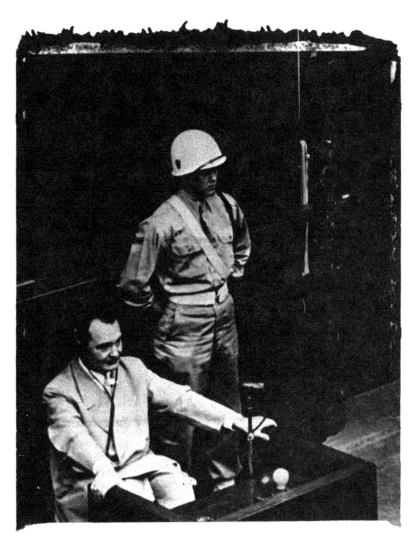

Göring in the witness box at
the International Military
Tribunal trial of war criminals
at Nuremberg

other defendants did. When asked, for example, why so many Germans had blindly followed Hitler, he replied that there wasn't anybody who had defied the Führer—not above ground, anyway.

On October 1, 1946, the tribunal pronounced sentence. Göring and eleven other Nazis were sentenced to death by hanging. Göring was not expecting mercy, but he was dissatisfied with the method of execution. He begged to be shot by a firing squad—a soldier's punishment—rather than hanging, which was reserved for common criminals. His request was denied.

But he still managed to cheat the hangman. On the night of October 15, 1946, just hours before he was to be executed, Göring took a fatal dose of cyanide poison that he had concealed in a jar of skin cream. He died within minutes and was cremated the next morning.

Hermann Göring was a man of tremendous energy. He was a bold and effective soldier in the First World War. Educated and far more cultured

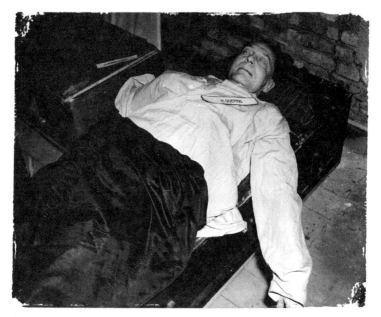

The body of Göring after he
committed suicide in prison
following the International
Military Tribunal in Nuremberg

than many of the men he spent his adult life
with, he had a highly cultivated sense of
personal honor that made him a devoted friend
and fearsome enemy.

Yet his honor extended only to those he
gave his loyalty to. In the First World War, that
was the German kaiser; after the war, it was
Adolf Hitler. His intense devotion to the

German dictator entangled him in schemes that no man of real honor would ever have allowed himself to participate in. He regularly betrayed friends and associates, even other Nazis—fatally, in the case of the Night of the Long Knives and on other occasions.

His honor was a tool of his ambition. Göring had jealously guarded his close association with the Führer, and ruthlessly worked to eliminate or undermine anyone else that got close to Hitler. He built up a personal empire of government agencies, not to help the people of Germany, but to increase his own power. And he helped instigate the loathsome policies of the Nazis toward the Jews and the conquered peoples of Europe. The blood of millions was on his hands.

Robert Jackson, the American prosecutor at the Nuremberg trial, summed up Göring's career:

He was half militarist and half gangster. He stuck a pudgy finger in every pie ... He was equally adept at massacring opponents and at framing scandals to get rid of stubborn generals. He built up the Luftwaffe and hurled it at his defenseless neighbors. He was among the foremost in harrying the Jews out of the land.

Göring once told his captors that he expected that in fifty years, there would be statues—even if they were only little ones—of Hermann Göring in every house in Germany. Today, Auschwitz prison camp is a museum to the memory of the six million who died in the Holocaust, the only fitting memorial to the man who did so much to bring about their deaths.

Timeline

January 1, 1893
Hermann Göring is born in Rosenheim, Bavaria, in southern Germany.

1914–1918
World War I. Göring distinguishes himself as a fighter pilot in the new German air force.

1922 Göring marries Carin von Flacknow, daughter of a Swedish nobleman.

1923 Göring leaves Germany and goes into exile in the wake of the failure of the Nazis' attempt to take over the Bavarian government.

1927 A general political amnesty enables Göring to return to Germany.

1928 Göring elected to the Reichstag, the German parliament.

1934 Hitler assumes dictatorial powers in Germany.

1935 Göring becomes head of the Luftwaffe, the German air force. Germany institutes the Nuremberg Laws, stripping Jewish citizens of their rights.

1939   Luftwaffe leads assault on Poland, beginning World War II.

1940   The Luftwaffe fails to win the Battle of Britain.

1941   Germany invades Russia.

1943   Allies begin "round-the-clock" bombing of German cities.

1944   German troops retreat from Russian soil, and Germany goes on the defensive. American and British forces land in Normandy, France, opening up a second front against the Germans.

May 9, 1945
Göring surrenders to American troops.

October 1, 1946
An Allied court at Nuremberg sentences Göring to death by hanging. On October 15, cheating the hangman, Göring takes a fatal dose of cyanide and dies.

Glossary

Allies
In World War II, Great Britain, France, the Soviet Union, and (after 1941) the United States.

Anschluss
German for "unification"; refers to the unification of Austria and Germany that was specifically forbidden by the Treaty of Versailles.

Auschwitz
Largest and most infamous of the German extermination camps; located near the town of Oswiecim in central Poland.

Blitzkrieg
German for "lightning war"; refers to the combined air and tank attacks perfected by the Germans during World War II.

Einsatzkommando
"Special Action Commandos"; killing squads organized by the SS to exterminate Jews in the conquered regions of eastern Europe.

field marshall
The highest rank in most European armies, above even
a full general.

Final Solution (Endlösung)
The Nazi plan to exterminate the Jews of Europe.

Führer
German word for "leader"; Hitler's title while he was dictator
of Germany.

general government
Nazi puppet government set up in central Poland, between
the sections added directly to Germany and the parts
occupied by the Soviet Union.

Gestapo
The *Geheime Staatspolizei,* or Secret State Police; the branch
of the SS responsible for undercover espionage against
enemies of the Nazis.

Kristallnacht
The "Night of Broken Glass," November 9, 1938, when the
Nazis rampaged throughout Germany, destroying Jewish
businesses and synagogues.

Luftwaffe
The German air force in World War II.

National Socialism
Nazism; the theories of the Nazi Party as dictated by
Adolf Hitler.

NSDAP
The German initials for the National Socialist German
Workers' Party, the official name of the Nazi Party.

rasputitsa
The rainy season of fall and spring in Russia.

SA (Sturmabteilung)
The Storm Troopers or Brownshirts, a collection of thugs and
criminals that were the original enforcement branch of
the Nazi Party until replaced by the SS.

SD (Sicherheitsdienst)
The secret police division of the SS.

SS (Schutzstaffel)
The black-uniformed elite of the Nazi Party that controlled
the Gestapo and ran the concentration and
extermination camps.

Treaty of Versailles
Treaty that ended World War I and imposed harsh terms
on Germany.

Vichy, France
The Nazi puppet government of the southern (originally
unoccupied) part of France under the control of Marshall
Henri Petain.

western democracies
Great Britain, France, and the United States.

For Further Reading

Adler, David. *We Remember the Holocaust.* New York: Henry Holt, 1989.

Ayer, Eleanor. *The United States Holocaust Memorial Museum: America Keeps the Memory Alive.* Parsippany, NJ: Dillon Press, 1995.

Chaiken, Miriam. *A Nightmare in History: The Holocaust, 1933-45.* New York: Clarion Books, 1987.

Fox, Anne L., and Eva Abraham-Podietz, eds. *Ten Thousand Children: True Stories Told by Children Who Escaped the Holocaust on the Kindertransport.* West Orange, NJ: Behrman House, 1998.

Frank, Anne. *Diary of a Young Girl: The Definitive Edition.* New York: Doubleday, 1995.

Kallen, Stuart A. *The Nazis Seize Power, 1933-41.* Edina, MN: Abdo Publishing Co., 1994.

Mosely, Leonard. *The Reich Marshall.* Garden City, NY: Doubleday & Company, Inc., 1974.

Rice, Earle Jr. *Nazi War Criminals.* San Diego: Lucent Books, 1997.

Rochman, Hazel, and Darlene Z. McCampbell, eds. *Bearing Witness: Stories of the Holocaust.* New York: Orchard Books, 1995.

Wiesel, Elie. *Night.* New York: Bantam Books, 1982.

For Advanced Readers

Gilbert, Martin. *The Holocaust: A History of Jews in Europe During the Second World War.* New York: Henry Holt & Co., 1985.

Overy, R. J. *Göring: The Iron Man.* London: Routledge & Kegan Paul, 1984.

Rogasky, Barbara. *Smoke and Ashes: The Story of the Holocaust.* New York: Holiday House, Inc., 1988.

Sanford, William R., Ron Knapp, and Carl R. Green. *American Generals of World War II.* Berkeley Heights, NJ: Enslow Publishers, 1998.

Shirer, William L. *The Rise and Fall of the Third Reich.* New York: Simon & Schuster, Inc., 1959.

Spiegelman, Art. *Maus: A Survivor's Tale. Part I: My Father Bleeds History.* New York: Pantheon Books, 1986.

———. *Maus: A Survivor's Tale. Part II: And Here My Troubles Began.* New York: Pantheon Books, 1991.

For More Information

Simon Wiesenthal Center and Museum of
   Tolerance
9760 West Pico Boulevard
Los Angeles, CA 90035
(800) 900-9036
Web site: http://www.wiesenthal.com

Survivors of the Shoah Visual History Foundation
P.O. Box 3168
Los Angeles, CA 90078-3168
(818) 777-4673
Web site: http://www.vhf.org

United States Holocaust Memorial Museum
100 Raoul Wallenberg Place SW
Washington, DC 20024-2126
(202) 488-0400
(202) 488-0406 (TTY-TDD)
Web site:http://www.ushmm.org

Web Sites

The American Experience: America and the
   Holocaust
http://www.pbs.org/wgbh/amex/holocaust

Anne Frank House Homepage
http://www.annefrank.nl

Anti-Defamation League, Braun Holocaust
   Institute
http://www.adl.org/frames/front_braun.html

Holocaust Memorial Center
http://www.holocaustcenter.org/holocaust.shtml

Illustrated History of the Holocaust
http://www.fatherryan.org/holocaust

Who's Who in Nazi Germany
http://zelda.thomson.com/routledge/who/
   germany/intro.html

Index

Credits

About the Author

Fred Ramen is a freelance writer who lives in New York City.

Photo Credits

Cover image © United States Holocaust Memorial Museum (USHMM). Pp. 9, 13, 27, 30, 79 © USHMM; p. 14 © Friedrich Ebert Stiftung/USHMM; p. 20 © Kampf und Sieg der NSDAP; p. 22 © James Sanders/USHMM; p. 25 Nordrhein-West Faelisches; p. 35 © Deutsches Historisches Museum/USHMM; p. 38 © Nederlands Instituut voor Oorlogsdocumentatie/USHMM; pp. 46, 57, 93 © Yad Vashem Photo Archives/USHMM; p. 49 © Richard A. Ruppert/USHMM; p. 63 © Deutsches Historisches Museum; p. 69 YIVO Institute for Jewish Research/USHMM; pp. 71, 74 © National Archive/USHMM; p. 87 © Muzej Revolucije Narodnosti Jugoslavije/USHMM; p. 91 © Marie Hess Brandes/USHMM; p. 96 © William O. McWorkman/USHMM; p. 98 © Jerrold Siegal/USHMM

Design and Layout

Cynthia Williamson